Search Engine Made Simple:

A Practical Guide to SEO for SMEs

(Edition: May 2023)

By: Josee Ha

About the Authur

Josee Ha is an experienced SEO expert specializes in search engine optimization, Wikipedia and consultant in marketing strategy.   With over a decade of experience in the industry, Josee has helped numerous clients improve their online visibility and drive more traffic to their websites through effective SEO strategies.

She is also a finding committee of young entrepreneur association and still acting as consultant.   As a passionate educator, she frequently shares her knowledge and insights through articles, workshops, and training programs.

Introduction

Welcome to the book.

"Search Engine Made Simple: A Practical Guide to SEO for SMEs" is a comprehensive guide to search engine optimization written by SEO expert Josee Ha. This book is designed to help small and medium-sized enterprises (SMEs) improve their online visibility and attract more traffic to their websites through effective SEO strategies.

The book is divided into five sections, each covering a different aspect of SEO. Section 1 provides an introduction to SEO and teaches readers how to set target keywords to improve their search engine rankings. Section 2 focuses on on-page optimization, covering topics such as optimizing website content, using images and videos, and ensuring mobile-friendliness. Section 3 covers off-page optimization, including building high-quality backlinks and leveraging social media. Section 4 is all about submission, covering topics such as submitting sitemaps to search engines and getting listed on directories. Finally, Section 5 covers maintenance and monitoring, teaching readers how to publish fresh content regularly and use analytics to monitor and improve their SEO efforts.

Throughout the book, Josee provides easy-to-follow lessons and practical tips that SMEs can implement right away to improve their search engine rankings. Her step-by-step approach makes SEO accessible to anyone, regardless of their technical expertise.

TABLE OF CONTENT

Lesson 1: Introduction to SEO

Search Engine Optimization (SEO) is the process of optimizing a website to improve its visibility and ranking on search engine result pages (SERPs).

Functions of a Website

This is very important for some companies that rely on their website, a form of online presence, in their business where it has multi-functions:

- provide information
- drive new customers
- build higher brand awareness
- improve credibility
- conduct actual sales
- provide after-sale services
- maintain customer relationship
- and ultimately drive more revenue.

This is especially true for small and media-size enterprises (SEMs) because this may be their major exposure to access a widening audience and potential customers. They also may not have the budget and resources as target corporations, who can hire dedicated SEO professionals and implement more advanced tactics. The purpose of this course is to help SME owners effectively utilize their resources and achieve good results in their website optimization.

Importance of SEO

SEO involves various techniques and strategies that aim to make a website more search engine-friendly, so that it can be easily discovered by users who are searching for relevant information or products online base on targeted keywords.

The ultimate goal of SEO is to drive more organic traffic to a website, which can lead to increased brand awareness, higher conversion rates, and improved business revenue.

A higher search ranking is the result of better website optimization. It may help a company's website to:
- increase its visibility
- drive organic traffic
- collect targeted sales leads
- seen as more authoritative and trustworthy
- improve user experience
- higher engagement
- higher conversion rates
- easier for users to find information
- create a more seamless and enjoyable browsing experience overall

Basic SEO Techniques

SEO encompasses both on-page and off-page optimization techniques.

On-page optimization refers primarily the website itself.   It involves optimizing the content and structure of a website, including the use of relevant keywords, meta tags, and other elements that search engines use to rank websites.

Off-page optimization, on the other hand, refers to factors outside the website. It involves building backlinks from other websites and leveraging social media to improve a website's authority and reputation.

In this course, we will cover the following basic steps to improve your website's SEO.   There are 5 sections with totally 13 lessons:

Section 1: Getting Started
    Lesson 1: Introduction to SEO
    Lesson 2: Setting Target Keywords
Section 2: On-Page Optimization
    Lesson 3: Optimizing Website Content
    Lesson 4: Utilizing Images and Videos
    Lesson 5: Ensuring Mobile-Friendliness
Lesson 6: Improving Loading Speed
    Lesson 7: Securing Access with SSL
Section 3: Off-Page Optimization
    Lesson 8: Building High-Quality Backlinks
    Lesson 9: Leveraging Social Media

Section 4: Submission
Section 5: Maintenance and Monitoring

SEO is a constantly evolving field, as search engines continually update their algorithms to provide more accurate and relevant search results to users. As a result, SEO requires ongoing effort and attention to ensure that a website remains optimized and competitive in search engine rankings.

What do you see from a search result?

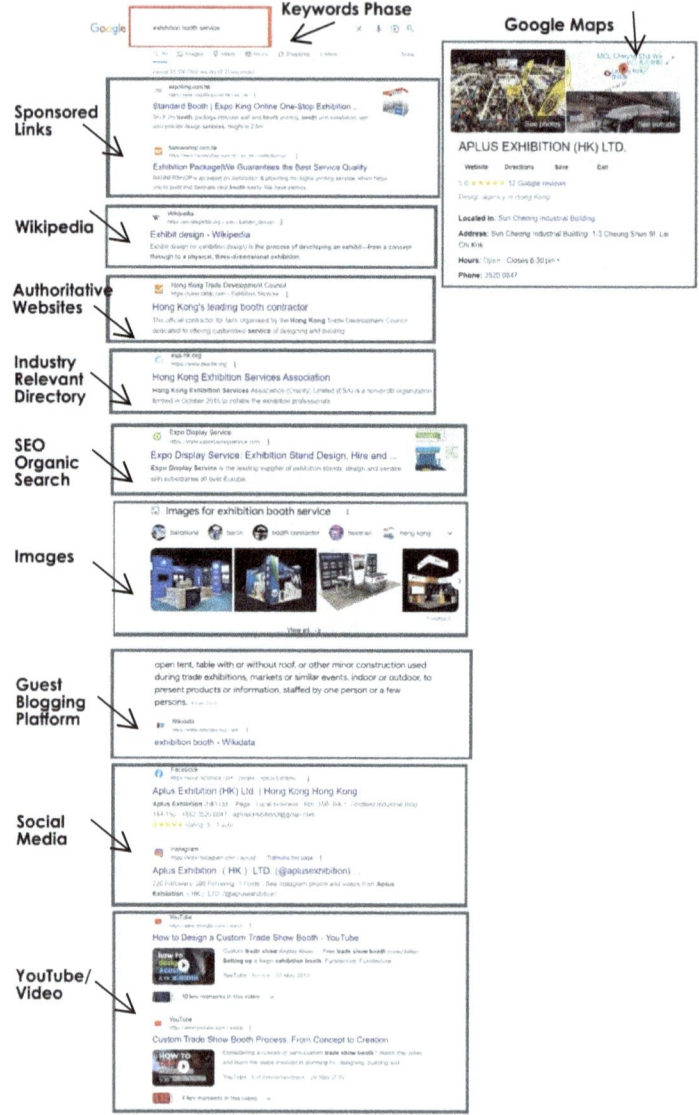

- Keywords Phase
- Google Maps
- Sponsored Links
- Wikipedia
- Authoritative Websites
- Industry Relevant Directory
- SEO Organic Search
- Images
- Guest Blogging Platform
- Social Media
- YouTube/ Video

Lesson 2: Setting Target Keywords

Identifying the keywords and phrases your target audience is searching for is a crucial step in optimizing your website content for search engines. Here are some steps to help you identify those keywords and phrases:

Define Your Target Audience

The internet is a vast ocean, you won't and can't drive everyone into your website.   This is unachievable, inefficient, and a waste of resources. You need to be very specific about the target audience or potential visitors to your website in order to provide the appropriate information, echo and get their attention, match with their expectations, and sell them the right product or services.

Before you start researching keywords, you need to have a clear understanding of the target audience of your website.

Some examples are:
Age:
Gender:
Location:
Occupation:
Interests:

Education level:
Pain points:
Surfing habits
Other demographic data:

Most important is the "pain points", their problem, their need, or their desire, because you or your website is about to give him/her the solution.

Imagine a real person in front of you, the dream customer you want: what is his/her age, work, family status, wealth level, when he/her surf on the web, how he/her travel around, what language he/her uses and etc. This helps you define your target in more detail. The clearer the picture, the more specific your target and the more effective your search optimization goes.

Conduct Keyword Research:

Keyword is the center of your SEO because this is the words and phrases your target audience is searching for. Only choosing the appropriate keywords enables your website to be displayed in any search result, let alone the ranking.

Keyword research tools:

There are many keyword research tools available, such as Google Keyword Planner,

Ahrefs, SEMrush, and Moz. These tools will help you identify the keywords and phrases that your target audience is searching for.

Google Keyword Planner:

1. Go to Google Keyword Planner: https://ads.google.com/home/tools/keyword-planner/
    Sign in using your Google Ads account. If you don't already have an account, create a new account for free.

2. Click on "Discover new keywords" and enter a product or service related to your business in the "Your product or service" field.

3. Enter your landing page URL or select your product category.

4. Select your target country and language.

5. Enter relevant keywords or phrases related to your product or service in the "Enter keywords" box. You can also upload a CSV file of keywords.

6. Click on "Get Results" to generate a list of related keywords and their search volume.

7. Review the list of keywords and sort by relevance, search volume, or competition.

8. Look for long-tail keywords with moderate search volume (say 2000 - 8000 search per month) and low competition that are closely related to your product or service.

9. Use this keyword phase to build your website around it .

Use long-tail keywords

Long-tail keywords are longer and more specific phrases that are less competitive and more targeted than shorter, more generic keywords. They are typically consist of three or more words.They are often used by people who are looking for specific information or products. Using long-tail keywords in your content can help you attract more targeted traffic to your website.

Serach volume

It's typically best to target keywords with a moderate to high search volume, while avoiding keywords that are either too broad or too niche.

Keywords with a very high search volume may be too competitive to target effectively, especially for smaller businesses or those with limited resources. Conversely, keywords with very low search volume may not generate enough traffic or interest to justify the effort and investment required to optimize for them.

A general guideline is to target keywords with at least a few hundred searches per month, up to several thousand or more for highly competitive industries.   Suggest to choose within range of **2000 - 8000 search per month**, depending on your keyword planner result.

Analyze your competitors

Using the above tools, look at the websites of your competitors and analyze the keywords they are targeting. This will give you a good idea of what keywords are relevant to your industry and what kind of content your target audience is interested in.

Google Search

One simple way to analyze your competitors is to search for the keywords you want to target and see what sites are ranking at the top of the search results. You can then visit those sites to see what kind of content they are producing and what keywords they are targeting.

Lesson 3: Optimizing Website Content

Use your target keywords in your website's meta title tags, meta descriptions, headers, and within the body of your content. Ensure that your content is high-quality, relevant, and provides value to your audience.

Use Keywords Throughout

Use keywords in page titles, headings, meta descriptions and
throughout your content, but be careful not to overuse them.

Page titles:

- Include your primary keyword at the beginning of the title
- Keep the title under 70 characters to ensure it is fully displayed in search results.
- Make sure the title accurately reflects the content of the page.

Headings:

- Use H1 tags for the main heading on each page.
- Use H2 and H3 tags for subheadings and section headings.
- Include your primary keyword in the H1 tag, if possible.

Meta descriptions:

- Write a compelling meta description that accurately summarizes the content of the page.
- Include your primary keyword in the meta description, if possible.
- Keep the meta description under 155 characters to ensure it is fully displayed in search results.

Content:

- Include your primary keyword in the first paragraph of your content.
- Use variations of your primary keyword throughout the content, but avoid overusing it.
- Focus on creating high-quality, engaging content that provides value to your audience.

WordPress plugin:

There are many WordPress plugins available to help with keyword optimization, including **Yoast SEO**, All in One SEO Pack, and Rank Math. These plugins can help you optimize your page titles, meta descriptions, and content for keywords, and provide guidance on best practices for on-page optimization.

Page 23

Lesson 4: Utilizing Images and Videos

Google and most search engines have a delegated section for pictures and videos on their front page.   So utilizing pictures, photos, and videos can be a powerful way to improve your website's visibility and engagement in search results.

Photo and Video Content

Here are some tips for optimizing your photos and videos for search:

Use descriptive filenames: Use descriptive filenames for your photos and videos that include relevant keywords and phrases. This can help search engines understand the content and context of your media.

Optimize alt tags and captions: Alt tags and captions provide additional metadata and context for your media. Use descriptive alt tags and captions that include relevant keywords and phrases to improve your visibility in search results.

Use high-quality media: Use high-quality photos and videos that are visually appealing and engaging. This can help improve user engagement and increase the likelihood of your content being shared and linked to. High quality does not mean high resolution which will slow down the loading speed (see next lesson), but are professional shots, with visual impact, relevant to the content, appealing to target customers, and may elicit sales.

Host your media on your own website: Host your photos and videos on your own website rather than relying on third-party hosting platforms. This can help improve your website's performance and loading speed and ensure that your content is easily accessible to search engines.

Share and promote your media: Share your photos and videos on social media and other platforms to increase their visibility and reach. Encourage others to share and link to your content to increase your website's authority and relevance in search results.

Lesson 5: Ensuring Mobile-Friendliness

Nowadays, people tend to use mobile phones to access the internet more than use a desktop as they are always on the move.   Optimize your website for mobile devices to improve user experience and search engine rankings.

Mobile Responsive Website

To ensure your website is mobile-friendly, there are several steps you can take:

Use a responsive design:

A responsive design ensures that your website adapts to different screen sizes and devices. This means your website will look great on desktops, laptops, tablets, and smartphones. Many WordPress themes are already designed to be responsive, but you can also use a plugin like **WPtouch** to create a mobile-specific version of your site.

Optimize your images:

Large images can slow down your site's loading times on mobile devices.

Resolution: The ideal resolution for photos on the web is 72 pixels per inch (ppi).

File size: Aim for a maximum file size of 100-200KB for most photos.

Dimensions: small thumbnail 150x150 pixels, larger full-width banner 1920x1080 pixels.

Compression: Use an image optimization tool like Imagify, Smush, or Kraken.io to compress your images and reduce their file size without sacrificing quality.

Simplify your navigation:

Mobile users have less screen real estate to work with, so it's important to simplify your navigation and make it easy for users to find what they're looking for. Keep your menu items to a minimum, and use clear, concise labels.

Use clear, easy-to-read fonts:

Some fonts may be difficult to read on a small screen. Use a font that is easy to read on both desktop and mobile devices, and make sure the font size is large enough to be legible on a small screen.

Font type: Sans-serif fonts like Arial, Verdana, and Helvetica are   more readable on screens

Font size: body text 16 pixels, headings and subheadings may need to be larger to stand out.

Line spacing: 1.5 or 1.6 is recommended for body text.

Contrast: the contrast between the font color and the background color is high enough to make the text easily readable.

Consistency: Use a consistent font and font size throughout the website to avoid confusion and make the site easier to navigate.

Test your site on multiple devices:

To ensure your site is truly mobile-friendly, test it on multiple devices, including smartphones and tablets. This will help you identify any issues and make sure your site is optimized for all mobile users.

WordPress plugins:

To help with mobile optimization, **WPtouch** is a popular option that allows you to create a mobile-specific version of your site. Other plugins like Jetpack and Autoptimize can also help improve your site's performance on mobile devices.

Lesson 6: Improving Loading Speed

Website visitors tend to have very little patience when it comes to slow loading speeds. In general, most users expect a website to load within 2-3 seconds, and will often leave the site if it takes longer than that. Study shows that for every additional second of page load time, the likelihood of a user bouncing increases by 123%.

Improve your Website's Loading Speed:

Optimize your website's loading speed images, compress files, minify CSS and JavaScript, and use a content delivery network (CDN) to speed up your website.

Optimize your website's images:

Large images can significantly slow down your website's loading times. Use an image optimization tool like Imagify, Smush, or Kraken.io to compress your images and reduce their file size without sacrificing quality.

Compress files:

Compressing your website's files, including HTML, CSS, and JavaScript, can also help reduce loading times. Use a tool like Gzip to compress your files and make them smaller.

Minify CSS and JavaScript:

Minifying your CSS and JavaScript files removes unnecessary white space and comments, which can help reduce file size and improve loading times. Use a tool like Minify or UglifyJS to minify your files.

Use a content delivery network (CDN):

A CDN distributes your website's files across multiple servers around the world, which can help improve loading times for users in different geographic locations. Popular CDNs include Cloudflare, MaxCDN, and Amazon CloudFront.

Use a caching plugin:

Caching plugins like WP Super Cache or W3 Total Cache can help improve loading times by storing a copy of your website's files on the user's device, reducing the need to download them from the server.

Limit the use of plugins:

Too many plugins can slow down your website's loading speed. Only use plugins that are essential to the functionality of your website, and make sure to delete any unused plugins.

Lesson 7: Securing Access with SSL

Search engines prioritize websites that are secure and protect user data. Make sure your website has an SSL certificate and is using HTTPS, and take steps to prevent hacking and other security threats.

Ensure Security

Ensuring the security of your website is important to protect your website and its users from potential threats and get a higher search ranking. Here are some steps you can take to improve your website's security:

Use SSL:

SSL (Secure Sockets Layer) is a security protocol that encrypts data transmitted between your website and its users. Using SSL ensures that any sensitive information, such as passwords and credit card numbers, is transmitted securely. Most web hosts offer SSL certificates, and you can also use a plugin like **Let's Encrypt** or **Really Simple SSL** to add SSL to your website.

Use strong passwords:

Use strong passwords for all user accounts on your website, including your own. A strong password should be at least 12 characters long and include a mix of letters, numbers, and symbols.

Keep your software updated:

Keep your website's software, including your content management system (CMS) and plugins, up to date to ensure that known security vulnerabilities are fixed.

Use security plugins:

Security plugins like Wordfence or **Jetpack** can help protect your website from malicious attacks and provide real-time monitoring and alerts.

Limit login attempts:

Limit the number of login attempts allowed on your website to prevent brute-force attacks. You can use a plugin like Login LockDown or **Jetpack** to limit login attempts.

Wordpress plugin:

If you don't have an SSL certificate, you can use a plugin like Let's Encrypt or Really Simple SSL to add SSL to your website. These plugins are easy to use and can help ensure that your website is secure and trusted by users and search engines.

- Install and activate the Really Simple SSL plugin from the WordPress plugin repository.

- Once activated, the plugin will automatically detect whether your site has an SSL certificate installed. If SSL is detected, the plugin will prompt you to activate SSL by clicking the "Activate SSL" button.

- If SSL is not detected, you will need to provide the plugin with the location of your CRT file, private key, and Certificate Authority Bundle (if applicable) in order to activate SSL. You can do this by going to Settings > SSL in the WordPress dashboard, and following the prompts to enter your SSL certificate information.

- After activating SSL, it's important to check your website to ensure that all pages and resources are loading correctly and that there are no mixed content warnings or errors. You can use tools like the SSL Check or SSL Server Test to verify that your SSL certificate is installed correctly and that your site is fully secure.

Lesson 8: Building High-Quality Backlinks

Building backlinks is the most important part of off-page optimization in SEO because they signal to search engines like Google that other websites consider your content to be valuable and relevant.

Inbound and Outbound Links

Backlinks, aka inbound links, are links from other websites that point to your website.

Outbound links are links from your website to other websites.

Search engines consider both inbound and outbound links when assessing the quality and relevance of a website.

Acquire High-Quality Backlinks

A backlink is essentially a link from one website to another, and search engines use these links to help determine the authority and credibility of a website. Acquire backlinks from high-authority websites in your niche to increase your website's authority and improve your search engine rankings.

Authoritative websites:

In terms of the quality of backlinks, links from authoritative websites like government (.gov), educational (.edu), or media outlets can be particularly valuable, as they are often considered trusted sources of information.

Relevance in the industry:

However, the quality of a backlink also depends on the relevance of the linking website to your website's content. A backlink from a relevant and authoritative website in your industry or niche is generally more valuable than a backlink from an unrelated website.

Quality over quantity:

It's also important to note that the quantity of backlinks is not as important as the quality. It's better to have a few high-quality backlinks from authoritative websites than many low-quality backlinks from irrelevant or spammy websites.

Blog Platforms

While there are many different blog platforms out there, some popular options for backlinking purposes include:

Guest blogging platforms:

These platforms are high-authority websites can be great for guest blogging and establishing backlinks. By writing quality blogs on these platforms, you can include link to your own website:

Medium: https://medium.com/
HubPages: https://hubpages.com/
LinkedIn: https://www.linkedin.com/

Industry-Specific Blogs

Look for blogs that cover topics related to your industry or niche and offer guest posting opportunities. For example, if you're in the tech industry, you might want to target blogs like TechCrunch or Wired.

TechCrunch: https://techcrunch.com/
Wired: https://www.wired.com/
Mashable: https://mashable.com/
Entrepreneur: https://www.entrepreneur.com/

Resource Directories:

Resource directories like Wikihow, HowStuffWorks, and About.com can be great places to establish backlinks if you have useful, informative content that fits their guidelines.

Wikihow: https://www.wikihow.com/

HowStuffWorks:
https://www.howstuffworks.com/
About.com: https://www.about.com/

Niche-Specific Forums:

If there are forums related to your niche or industry, you can participate in discussions and link back to your website when appropriate.

Reddit: https://www.reddit.com/
Quora: https://www.quora.com/
Stack Overflow: https://stackoverflow.com/

Outbound Links

Outbound links can also help improve SEO by providing value to your website's visitors and signaling to search engines that your website is a trusted and authoritative source of information. Here are a few ways that outbound links can help with SEO:

Providing value to your audience:

Outbound links to relevant and authoritative websites can provide additional value to your website's visitors by directing them to additional resources or information related to your content.

Building relationships:

Outbound links to other websites can help you build relationships with other website owners and bloggers in your industry or niche. This can lead to opportunities for guest blogging, link exchanges, or other collaborations that can help improve your website's visibility and authority.

Signaling to search engines:

Outbound links can help search engines understand the context and relevance of your website's content. By linking to other relevant and authoritative websites, you can signal to search engines that your website is a trusted source of information in your industry or niche.

Use strategically:

However, it's important to use outbound links strategically and avoid over-linking or linking to low-quality or spammy websites. Make sure that the outbound links on your website are relevant, valuable, and add to the user experience.

Use Internal Linking

Internal linking is the practice of linking to other pages on your website within your content. This can help improve the user experience and also helps search engines understand the structure and hierarchy of your website.

Lesson 9: Leveraging Social Media

Social media can be a valuable tool for SEO, as it can help increase your website's visibility, drive traffic, and provide social signals that can influence search engine rankings.

Promote Website on Social Media

Here are some tips for optimizing the use of social media to promote your website content:

Choose the right platforms:

Different social media platforms have different strengths and audiences.   Focus on the social media platforms that are most relevant to your industry or niche and where your target audience is most active. This will help ensure that your social media efforts are targeted and effective. Here are examples of popular social media:

Facebook: Facebook has a large user base, making it a good choice for businesses with a broad target audience. It can be effective for businesses in a variety of industries, including retail, hospitality, and services.

Instagram: Instagram is a highly visual platform that is well-suited for businesses that can showcase their products or services through images and videos. It is particularly popular with younger audiences and is a good choice for businesses in industries such as fashion, beauty, and food.

Twitter: Twitter is a fast-paced platform that is well-suited for businesses that want to engage with their audience in real-time and share timely news or updates. It is popular with journalists, influencers, and thought leaders, and can be effective for businesses in industries such as media, tech, and politics.

LinkedIn: LinkedIn is a professional networking platform that is well-suited for businesses in B2B industries. It can be effective for building professional relationships, sharing industry news and insights, and promoting thought leadership.

YouTube: YouTube is a video-sharing platform that is well-suited for businesses that want to share informative or instructional videos with their audience. It can be effective for businesses in industries such as education, technology, and entertainment.

Pinterest: Pinterest is a visual discovery platform and suitable for businesses that want to showcase their products or services through images and videos. It is particularly popular with female audiences and can be effective for businesses in industries such as art and craft, fashion, beauty, and home decor.

Optimize your profiles:

Make sure your social media profiles are fully filled out and include a link to your website. Use relevant keywords in your profile descriptions and hashtags to help improve your visibility in social media search results.

Link content to your website:

Share high-quality, informative, consistent to your branding, and engaging content on your social media channels that links back to your website. This can help drive traffic to your website and improve your search engine rankings.

Engage with your audience:

Engage with your audience on social media by responding to comments and messages and encouraging discussion. This can help build relationships and increase engagement, which can improve your social signals and search engine rankings.

Use social media advertising:

Consider using social media advertising to promote your content and drive traffic to your website. Social media advertising can be a cost-effective way to reach a targeted audience and increase your visibility.

Integrate Social Media in Website

On the other side of promoting your website in social media, integrating your website with social media also can help improve your social signals and drive traffic to your website. Here are some on-page optimizations you can make to better integrate your website with social media:

Add social sharing buttons:

Add social sharing buttons to your website to make it easy for visitors to share your website content on their own social media. Under Jetpack plugin, you can add sharing buttons (under Sharing) to your posts and pages automatically.

Add social media links:

Add links to your social media profiles on your website to encourage visitors to follow you and join your page or groups on social media. This can increase future interaction them, leading to higher brand loyalty.

Use Open Graph tags:

Open Graph tags are a type of meta tag that allows you to control how your content appears when shared on social media platforms like Facebook and Twitter. By optimizing your Open Graph tags, you can ensure that your content looks great when shared on social media and includes all the relevant information. Here are steps on how to use Open Graph tags:

Determine which pages or content on your website you want to optimize for social media. This may include blog posts, product pages, or other types of content.

Identify the key elements of your content that you want to highlight on social media. This may include the title, description, image, and other relevant information.

Add the appropriate Open Graph tags to the HTML code of your web pages. Each Open Graph tag should include a specific piece of information, such as the title, description, or image URL. Here are some examples of common Open Graph tags:

og:title: The title of your content
og:description: A brief description of your content
og:image: The URL of the image you want to display on social media
og:url: The URL of the page containing your content
og:type: The type of content (e.g. article, product, video)

Test your Open Graph tags using a tool like the Facebook Sharing Debugger or the Twitter Card Validator. These tools will show you how your content will appear on social media and alert you to any issues with your Open Graph tags.

Adjust your Open Graph tags as needed based on the results of your testing. You may need to adjust the size or format of your images, tweak your description or title, or make other changes to optimize your content for social media.

Use schema markup:

Schema markup is a type of structured data that helps search engines understand the content on your website. By using schema markup to identify your social media profiles, you can improve your visibility and help search engines understand your social media presence.

YouTube channel

On the first page of Google always include a section for video that comes from YouTube. Having a YouTube channel can be a powerful way to improve your website's visibility and engagement in search results, as YouTube is the world's second-largest search engine and a popular platform for video content. Here are some tips for using a YouTube channel to improve your website's SEO:

Optimize your videos for search:

Use relevant keywords and phrases in your video titles, descriptions, and tags to improve your visibility in YouTube search results. To help with your website search result, it is preferable to have a consistent keyword on both.   Use high-quality visuals and engaging content to keep users watching and increase engagement.

Embed videos on your website:

Embed your YouTube videos on your website to increase engagement and dwell time on your website. It also helps to increase possible subscribers to your YouTube page to increase interaction and improve customer retention and brand loyalty.   This can also help improve your website's relevance and authority in search results.

Link to your website:

Use annotations and calls-to-action in your videos to encourage users to engage with your content and visit your website. Include links to your website and other relevant content to drive traffic and improve engagement.

Note that Google and YouTube use different algorithms so YouTube channel with high subscriber does not have a direct relation to your website SEO. However, having your YouTube channel provides another possible exposure of your business, allowing a cross-linkage between the website and channel and driving traffic both ways. Also high-quality and engaging video lead to more backlinks and social shares, which are important ranking factors for Google search results.

Lesson 10: Submitting Sitemap to Search Engines

Theoretically having your website searchable is automatic.   Search engines use automated web crawlers to discover and index web pages, and they may eventually find all of the pages on your website.   However, there are about 2 billion websites on the internet, and thousands of new websites are launched every day making this a long and uncertain process.

Sitemap

Submitting a sitemap can help search engines understand the structure of your website and the relationships between different pages. This can help improve the indexing and ranking of your pages, especially if your website has a complex structure or if some pages are difficult to discover through normal crawling.

A sitemap is a file that lists all the pages on your website and helps search engine crawlers understand the structure of your site. Submit your sitemap to Google Search Console and other search engines to help them find and index your pages.

If you are using WordPress, then it by default generates a sitemap that includes all of the posts, pages, and other content on your website, and   is updated automatically whenever you add or remove content.

In addition to the built-in sitemap functionality, there are many third-party plugins available for WordPress that can help you optimize your sitemap for search engines and customize the content that is included. Some popular sitemap plugins for WordPress include Yoast SEO, All in One SEO Pack, and Google XML Sitemaps.

Submit to Google Search

To submit your website to Google Search Console, follow these steps:

1. Go to Google Search Console (https://search.google.com/search-console).

2. Sign in with your Google account or create a new account if you don't have one.

3. Click on the "Add Property" button in the top left corner of the page.

4. Enter your website's URL in the "Enter website domain" field and click "Continue."

5. Verify ownership of your website using one of the available methods (HTML file upload, HTML tag, Google Analytics, or Google Tag Manager).

6. Once your ownership is verified, you can access the Google Search Console dashboard and start monitoring your website's performance and optimizing it for search engines.

Submit to Bing (and Yahoo) Search

To submit a sitemap to Bing's Webmaster Tools:

1. Go to the Bing Webmaster Tools
   https://www.bing.com/toolbox/webmaster

2. Sign in with your Microsoft account.

3. Click on the website you want to submit a sitemap for.

4. Once you are on the dashboard for your website, click   on the "Sitemaps" option under "Configure My Site" in   the left-hand menu.

5. Click on the "Submit a Sitemap" button on the Sitemaps   page.

6. Enter the URL of your sitemap in the "Submit a Sitemap"   box. The URL should be the full path to your sitemap   file, such as https://www.example.com/sitemap.xml.

7. Click on the "Submit" button to submit your sitemap to Bing.

8. Bing will then process your sitemap and start to crawl your website.

9. You can check the status of your sitemap submission by returning to the Sitemaps page in Bing Webmaster Tools.

Yahoo:

Yahoo search results are powered by Bing, so if you've already submitted your website to Bing, it should be included in Yahoo's search results as well.

Lesson 11: Getting Listed on Directories

Apart from submitting your website sitemap to search engines, there are a number of well-done directories, Wikipedia, Google Maps and ChatGPT that can help increase exposure and/or establish backlinks.

Submit to Directories

Choose the ones that are appropriate to your geographic location, industry and products

Craigslist: Craigslist is a popular online platform where users can post classified ads for items, services, and jobs. It's a great platform for local SEO and can help drive traffic to your website, especially if you're a small business or service provider in a local area. Craiglist is basically for USA market but it may be helpful for backlink even your business is outside the States: Link : https://www.craigslist.org/

DuckDuckGo: DuckDuckGo is a popular search engine that emphasizes privacy and doesn't track user data. Link : https://duckduckgo.com/

Yelp: Yelp is a popular directory for local businesses, where customers can leave reviews and ratings. Link: https://www.yelp.com/

TripAdvisor: TripAdvisor is a directory for travel and hospitality businesses, where customers can leave reviews and ratings. Link: https://www.tripadvisor.com/

YellowPages: YellowPages is an online directory for local businesses, including phone numbers and addresses. Link: https://www.yellowpages.com/

Angie's List: Angie's List is a directory for home services businesses, where customers can leave reviews and ratings. Link: https://www.angieslist.com/

Maps for Physical Shop

If you are selling your products and services in a physical location of a shop, office, or other venues, by submitting your website and business detail. say Google Maps, improve your local SEO, and increase your visibility in local search results which can be easier found by potential customers. Make sure to keep your business information up-to-date and respond to customer reviews to further improve your online reputation.

Apple Maps:

Apple Maps is a mapping service that includes listings for local businesses. Link : https://maps.apple.com/

Google Map:

Google My Business (GMB), which will allow your business to appear on Google Maps and in local search results. Here's how to submit your business to Google My Business:

1. Go to https://www.google.com/business/ and sign in with your Google account.

2. Click "Add location" and enter your business's name and address.

3. Choose a business category that accurately describes your business.

4. Verify your business by phone, email, or postcard.

5. Once your business is verified, complete your business profile by adding photos, hours of operation, and other relevant information.

6. Monitor and manage your business listing to ensure that the information is accurate and up-to-date.

Wikipedia

If your business can be listed on Wikipedia, it is almost certain you will be listed on the first page, if not the top rank, when people search for the correct keyword. Including your business in Wikipedia greatly help improve its online visibility and credibility, as Wikipedia is one of the most popular and authoritative websites on the internet.

However, it's important to note that not all businesses are eligible for inclusion in Wikipedia, and the inclusion process can be challenging and time-consuming.

To qualify for inclusion in Wikipedia, your business must meet certain notability guidelines, which are based on the significance and verifiability of your business in reliable, independent sources. Your business must have significant coverage in these sources, such as news articles, academic journals, or books, that are not affiliated with your business.

If you believe that your business meets the notability guidelines and would like to add it to Wikipedia, you can create a draft article and submit it for review by the Wikipedia community. However, it's important to note that the Wikipedia community is known for its strict standards and guidelines, and it can be difficult to have an article accepted.

ChatGPT

AI tools such as ChaptGPT of Open AI are getting increasingly important. It is said that people in the future may directly ask for information from AI, and skip going to search engines. While ChatGPT will soon be accepting plugins, you may want to let ChatGPT finds your website. However, note that references made from AI may not, and usually do not, include your website or your business name so may not help with your SEO. It will be your decision whether you believe the information from your website is worth to be referred in these AI tools.

To be included in ChatGPT, you need to edit robot.txt, which is a file tells a search engine where it is allowed to go on your website. You may use Yoast SEO plugin to do so: (https://yoast.com/help/how-to-edit-robots-txt-through-yoast-seo/)

1. Log in to your WordPress website.

2. When you're logged in, you will be in your 'Dashboard'.

3. Click on 'Yoast SEO' in the admin menu.

4. Click on 'Tools'.

5. Click on 'File Editor'.
(This menu will not appear if your WordPress install has disabled file editing. Please enable file editing or edit the file through FTP.)

6. Click the Create robots.txt file button.

7. Edit the file generated by Yoast SEO to include:

"User-agent: ChatGPT-User
Disallow: "

More Impact of AI to SEO

As Google and Bing may be launching new search result format, it's important you prepare your website to suit for increasing AI users.

Focus on user intent: Instead if traditional keyword phase, AI works more on prompts, a specific instruction or task given to a computer program or AI to generate a response or output. So you need to provide content according to the user's intention, i.e. the reason behind a user's search query. They can be looking for information, comparing options, reviewing your product or service, or reaffirming a buying decision.   Structure your content and use appropriate tone.

Use natural language and conversational tone: People are likely getting use to ask question, whether by text or even voice search, which is becoming increasingly popular.   Optimize your website's content for prompts and voice search, may help improve your visibility in search results. Use natural language and conversational tone in your content, and anticipate commons relevance and performance in search results.

Lesson 12: Publishing Fresh Content Regularly

Search engines prioritize websites that have updated information with regular new high-quality content. Maintaining a high ranking involve regularly publish of fresh, high-quality, and valuable content. A consistent practice not only improves your website's search engine rankings, it also increases your website's authority and your business as well.

Maintaining Fresh Content

Some points to be considered in your content updating :

Quality over quantity:

It's more important to create high-quality, informative, and engaging content than to publish a high volume of low-quality content. Focus on creating content that is relevant and provides value to your audience around your business, website theme, and keyword.

Consistency:

Consistency is key when it comes to SEO. Create a content calendar and stick to a regular publishing schedule, whether it's weekly, biweekly, or monthly. This will help signal to search engines that your website is active and relevant.

Frequency:

There is no one size fits as to how frequently you need to update your content.   It will depend on your business, your target customers, and certainly your resources.   However, you may make reference to your competition and their content strategy. If they are publishing new content frequently, you may need to increase your publishing frequency to stay competitive.

Stay Fresh and Current:

Search engines prioritize fresh and up-to-date content, so it's important to regularly update your website with new content. If you can echo your content with news, hot topics, or current events in your industry, they are helpful to draw attention with high searches for that period. Followed by smooth user experience and retention strategies, even a short spark of traffic helps you increase popularity in the long run.

WordPress Plugin

If you are WordPress for your website, there are several plugins that can help with writing new posts and even automate the publishing process. Here are a few examples:

Yoast SEO: Yoast SEO is a popular plugin that helps with on-page SEO optimization. It includes a content analysis tool that provides suggestions for optimizing your content for search engines.

Grammarly: Grammarly is a plugin that checks your content for grammar, spelling, and punctuation errors. It can help you catch mistakes and improve the quality of your writing.

CoSchedule: CoSchedule is a popular content marketing calendar and scheduling tool. It allows you to plan, organize, and schedule your content in advance and automate the publishing process.

Blog2Social: Blog2Social is a social media automation plugin that allows you to automatically publish your blog posts to your social media channels. It supports all major social media platforms and includes features for customizing your social media posts.

WP RSS Aggregator. WP RSS Aggregator is a plugin that allows you to import RSS feeds from other websites and automatically publish the content on your own website. This can be a useful way to feed prewritten content and automate the publishing process.

Lesson 13: Using Analytics to Monitor and Improve SEO

SEO is dynamic as your search ranking keep changing over time, due to change in visitors' interest, search volume, competition, search engine algorithm change, new rules, or social changes.   Always monitor your SEO performance to constantly Improve your SEO.

Google Analytics

Use tools like Google Analytics to monitor your website's traffic, track your keyword rankings, and identify areas for improvement in your SEO strategy.

Google Analytics is a free web analytics service offered by Google that allows you to track and analyze website traffic and user behavior. To make use of the tools, you need to include the tracking number on your website.   Here is how you do it:

1. Access to Google Analytics :
https://analytics.google.com/

2. You'll need to sign in to your Google account or create a new account if you don't already have one. This is called a Google Analytics 4 (GA4) account

3. Fill in Account Name: This is the name you want to give to your GA4 account. It should be unique and

descriptive, as it will be used to identify your account in Google Analytics.

4. Fill in Asset Name: For website SEO purposes, this refers to your   Website Name that you want to track with GA4.

5. Industry Category: This is the category that best describes your website or app. Select the category that is most relevant to your business or industry.

6. Website URL: This is the URL of your website or app that you want to track with GA4. Make sure to include the full URL, including the "http://" or "https://" prefix.

7. Reporting Time Zone: This is the time zone that you want to use for reporting in GA4. Select the time zone that is most relevant to your location or business.

8. Data Sharing Settings: Google Analytics offers various data-sharing options that allow you to share your data with other Google products and services. Choose the data-sharing settings that are most appropriate for your business and needs.

9. You will be displayed with some coding for manual installation.   Copy the codes and paste them into each page of your website you want to track.   Paste after <heading>

Wordpress Plugin

If you are using **Yoast SEO plugin**, you can simply enter your measurement ID (GA4), (also known as a property ID something like G-XXXXXXXXXX) in the plugin.   If you want to track all pages in the website, check "Enable Google Analytics tracking"   (Global Site Tag: gtag.js)they will do the job for you.

The Yoast SEO plugin includes built-in integration with Google Analytics, which allows you to track your website's traffic and user behavior without adding any additional code to your website.

To verify that your Google Analytics tracking is working properly, you can log in to your Google Analytics account and check your real-time reports to see if your website is being tracked correctly. You can also view your standard reports to analyze your website's traffic, user behavior, and other metrics.

Note that while the Yoast SEO plugin can help simplify the process of setting up Google Analytics on your website, you may still need to configure other settings in your Google Analytics account, such as goals, events, and custom dimensions, to fully customize your tracking and analyze your data effectively.

Using Analysis to Improve SEO

The information provided by Google Analytics are very useful for you to constantly improve SEO. Here are some functions for the information they provide:

Identify traffic sources: Use Google Analytics to identify where your website traffic is coming from, including search engines, social media, and other websites. This can help you determine which channels are most effective for driving traffic to your website.

Track user behavior: Use Google Analytics to track user behavior on your website, including pageviews, bounce rate, and time on site. This can help you identify areas for improvement and optimize your website for better user engagement.

Set up goals: Use Google Analytics to set up goals for your website, such as completing a form or making a purchase. This can help you track conversions and better understand the effectiveness of your website in achieving your business objectives.

Monitor site speed: Use Google Analytics to monitor your website's speed and identify areas for improvement. Site speed is an important factor in user experience and can also impact your search engine rankings.

Segment your data: Use Google Analytics to segment your data by demographics, location, and other factors to better understand your audience and tailor your website and marketing efforts to their needs.

Monitor mobile traffic: Use Google Analytics to monitor your website's mobile traffic and optimize your website for mobile devices. Mobile traffic is increasingly important and can have a significant impact on your website's success.

Remember, the algorithm of search engines is ever-changing, as well as many industry practices and resources.   Keeping yourself updated with the development and constantly reviewing your website SEO performance is vital for keeping ahead and ranking high.

Worksheet

Lesson 2: Setting Target Keywords

Define Target Audience of your website

Age:		
Gender:		
Location:		
Occupation:		
Interests:		
Education level:		
Pain points:		
other demographic data:		

Conduct Keyword Research

Google Keyword Planner:
https://ads.google.com/home/tools/keyword-planner/

Keyword Phase	Seach Volume /mth	Competition	Relevent	
1.				
2.				
3.				
4.				
5.				

Lesson 3: Optimizing Website Content

Add Common Used WordPress Plugins

	Yoast SEO	on-page SEO optimization, add robot.txt, add sitemap, add Google Anaylstics 4
	Jackpack	security, add social media sharing button, Verify site ownership with third-party services (Google, Bing, Pinterest, Facebook), limit login attempts
	WPtouch	mobile responsive website
	Smush	compress photo size
	Really Simple SSL	SSL

Lesson 8: Building High-Quality Backlinks

Sign up and post blogs into these platforms to establish backlinks:

Platforms	Account	Post
Medium		
HubPages		
Wikihow		

Lesson 9: Leveraging Social Media

Sign up accounts with these social media, update profile and add website links:

	Account	Profile update	Website linked	
Facebook				
Instagram				
Twitter				
LinkedIn				
Pinterest				
YouTube				

Lesson 10: Submitting Sitemap to Search Engines

☐ Submit to Google Search Console

☐ Submit to Bing Webmaster Tool

Lesson 11: Getting Listed on Directories

	Sumitted	
Craigslist:		
Google Maps		
ChatGPT robot.txt		

Lesson 13: Using Analytics to Monitor and Improve SEO

Set up Google Analytics account and include measurement ID (GA4) into website

☐ Google Analytics   G_____

~ Thank You ~

www.ingramcontent.com/pod-product-compliance
Lightning Source LLC
Chambersburg PA
CBHW070451220526
45466CB00004B/1800